FACT CAT

ROMAN BRITAIN

Izzi Howell

FACT CAT

Get your paws on this fantastic new mega-series from Wayland!

Join our Fact Cat on a journey of fun learning about every subject under the sun!

Published in paperback in Great Britain in 2016
Copyright © Wayland 2016

ISBN: 978 0 7502 9936 7
Dewey Number: 936.1'04-dc23
10 9 8 7 6 5 4 3 2 1

MIX
Paper from
responsible sources
FSC® C104740

Wayland
An imprint of Hachette Children's Group
Part of Hodder & Stoughton
Carmelite House
50 Victoria Embankment
London EC4Y 0DZ

An Hachette UK Company
www.hachette.co.uk
www.hachettechildrens.co.uk

A catalogue for this title is available from the British Library
Printed and bound in China

Produced for Wayland by
White-Thomson Publishing Ltd
www.wtpub.co.uk

Editor: Izzi Howell
Design: Rocket Design (East Anglia) Ltd
Fact Cat illustrations: Shutterstock/Julien Troneur
Other illustrations: Stefan Chabluk
Consultant: Kate Ruttle

Picture and illustration credits:
Corbis: Heritage Images 7 and 10, Stefano Bianchetti 14, The Print Collector 20; iStock: Anthony Brown 11b, BrettCharlton 12; Shutterstock: yahiyat (cover), Laurence Gough (title page), KKulikov 4, Regien Paassen 6, verityjohnson 8, stocksolutions 9, Laurence Gough 13, Iuri 15, Hein Nouwens 16, mountainpix 17t, cpaulfell 18, Andrei Nekrassov 19, ChameleonsEye 21; Stefan Chabluk: 5; Wikimedia: Walters Art Museum (acquired in 1930) 11t and 17b.

The author, Izzi Howell, is a writer and editor specialising in children's educational publishing.

The consultant, Kate Ruttle, is a literacy expert and SENCO, and teaches in Suffolk.

FACT CAT FACT

There is a question for you to answer on each spread in this book. You can check your answers on page 24.

CONTENTS

THE ROMAN EMPIRE

Nearly 3,000 years ago, the **population** of the Italian city of Rome started to grow. Rome became the most powerful city in Italy. The people from Rome (the Romans) began to control the whole country.

Many Roman buildings, such as the Colosseum, still stand in Italy today. In Roman times, people visited the Colosseum to watch **gladiator** fights.

Over the next 500 years, the Romans took control of many countries in Europe, the Middle East and North Africa. These countries followed Roman **laws** and spoke Latin, the Roman language. Even though their **empire** was large, the Romans always wanted more land to control.

This map shows the Roman Empire in 117CE, when the empire was at its largest.

BRITAIN
London

Atlantic Ocean

Caspian Sea

Black Sea

ITALY
Rome

Mediterranean Sea

☐ Roman Empire in 117CE

FACT CAT FACT

The Romans controlled an area that is divided into 54 countries today, from Portugal in the west to Iraq in the east. What was the Roman name for Portugal?

THE ROMANS ARRIVE IN BRITAIN

The Romans first tried to **invade** Britain in 55BCE. The **Celts**, who controlled Britain at that time, beat the Romans in battle. Nearly 100 years later, **Emperor** Claudius invaded Britain again. This time, the Romans **defeated** the Celts and began to take control of southern Britain.

We think that Roman soldiers wore armour like this. Emperor Claudius sent over 40,000 Roman soldiers to invade Britain in 43CE.

FACT CAT FACT

Emperor Claudius ordered that an elephant should be part of the army that invaded Britain. The Romans often used elephants in battles to scare their enemies.

After the Roman **invasion**, Britain became part of the Roman Empire. Romans from all over the empire came to Britain to live alongside the Celts. Some Celts were unhappy about being ruled by Romans. They tried to fight back but each time the Romans defeated them.

This drawing shows the Celts attacking the town of Londinium, known today as London. What was the name of the Celtic queen who led a **rebellion** against the Romans?

HADRIAN'S WALL

Northern Britain and Scotland were not part of the Roman Empire. Scottish **tribes** would sometimes attack Roman Britain. In 122CE, Emperor Hadrian decided to build a high wall across the north of England to control who could enter the country.

Hadrian's Wall was between five and six metres tall. It ran for nearly 120km from the east coast to the west coast of England.

Soldiers lived in forts along Hadrian's Wall. They **patrolled** up and down the wall to make sure nobody climbed over.

Parts of Hadrian's Wall can still be seen today. These are the remains of a milecastle, a type of small fort.

FACT CAT FACT

The Romans measured distance using the Roman mile. A Roman mile was the same as 1,000 steps. How long is a Roman mile in kilometres?

AROUND TOWN

The Romans built towns all over Britain, connected by straight roads. They built their new towns in the same style and layout as the towns in the rest of their empire. In the town centre, there was always a large open market called a **forum**. Town meetings took place in a **basilica**, next to the forum.

This is a drawing of the Roman town of Londinium. In Roman times, there was a wooden bridge across the River Thames.

forum

FACT CAT FACT

Londinium was one of the largest towns in Roman Britain. However, its population of 60,000 people is much smaller than the population of London today, which is 8.4 million people!

The Romans built shops, **temples** and **public baths** in their towns. Rich Romans went to the public baths several times a week to clean themselves and meet their friends. Public baths had hot, warm and cold baths and outdoor gyms.

To keep clean, the Romans would cover themselves in olive oil at the public baths and then get a **slave** to scrape off the oil and dirt using this tool, called a strigil.

The Roman baths in Bath are still standing today. What was the Roman name for the city of Bath?

HOUSES AND VILLAS

The Romans brought new ideas about house building to Britain. Celtic houses were made from wood, mud and straw. Roman houses were made from brick and stone.

These are the remains of a Roman house's central heating system. The floor was built on top of tall stones with an empty space below. Hot air was pumped into the empty space under the floor to keep the house warm.

In Roman towns, poor people lived in small houses with two or three rooms. Rich people lived in large townhouses. In the country, rich Romans built large stone **villas** on farms. Slaves worked on the farm and lived in small buildings nearby.

Roman villas often had decorated **mosaic** floors. Mosaics are made by placing small coloured tiles close together to make a picture or a pattern.

FACT CAT FACT

More Roman villas were built in southern Britain than in northern Britain. Can you find out the name of a British Roman villa that you can visit the ruins of today?

FOOD AND FEASTS

In Roman Britain, poor people ate mainly porridge, soup and bread. Only rich people could afford to buy meat. Poor women would take meals to the baker's shop to be cooked because many small houses didn't have kitchens.

Rich Romans enjoyed eating dishes such as peacock tongues and roasted dormice at fancy dinners prepared and served by slaves. What was dinner called in Roman times?

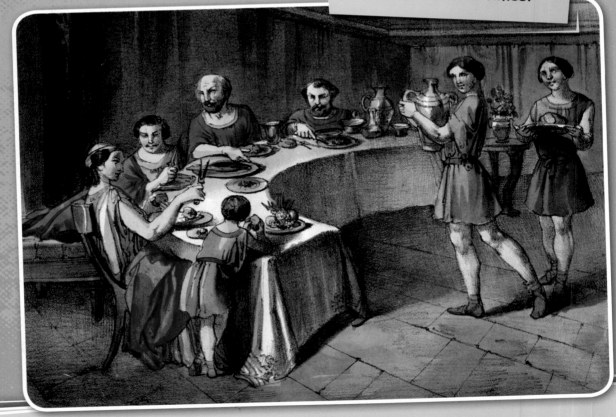

The Romans brought new fruit and vegetable seeds to Britain, such as celery and apples. These plants had never been grown in Britain before. The Romans also brought dried fruit, wine and olives to Britain from other countries in their empire.

The Romans imported olive oil and wine in clay containers called **amphorae**.

FACT CAT FACT

The Romans loved to add garum, a sauce made from rotten fish, to their food. They thought that it made their food taste better.

CLOTHES AND JEWELLERY

Rich Roman men in Britain, and across the Roman Empire, often wore **togas** – one long piece of cloth that was wrapped several times around the body. Ordinary men would wear cloth tunics, which were easier to move around in than togas.

This drawing shows a Roman man wearing a toga. Which materials were most Roman clothes made from?

FACT CAT FACT

The piece of cloth worn as a toga was 6m long! That's three times as long as a single bed!

Some Roman jewellery was useful, such as the metal brooches that men and women used to hold their clothes in place. Roman women also wore **expensive** gold necklaces, bracelets and rings to show how rich they were.

Mosaics show us the hairstyles that Roman women wore. Rich women had their hair plaited and curled by slave hairdressers called ornatrices.

These gold bracelets are made in the shape of snakes. The Romans believed that wearing snake-shaped jewellery would keep them safe from bad luck.

17

RELIGION

The Romans believed in many different gods and goddesses. The king of the Roman gods was Jupiter, who was also god of the sky. Jupiter was married to Juno, the goddess of marriage.

Some months are named after Roman gods. March is named after Mars, the god of war, and June is named after Juno.

trident

Neptune, the Roman god of the sea, is usually shown carrying a **trident**. How was Neptune related to the god Jupiter?

There were many **myths** about the Roman gods. Some myths were about the history of the gods and their special powers, such as Jupiter's power to throw a lightning bolt. Other myths told stories about gods coming to Earth to talk to humans.

This statue shows Romulus and Remus, the sons of the god Mars. One Roman myth tells that they were looked after by a wolf when they were children. The myth also says that Romulus **founded** the city of Rome.

THE END OF ROMAN BRITAIN

By the end of the 4th century, the Roman Empire was so big that it was difficult and expensive to control. Tribes of people from northern Europe started to attack countries in the west of the Roman Empire. Over time, the Romans lost land and their empire got smaller.

In 383CE, Roman soldiers began to leave Britain on ships. They sailed to other parts of the Roman Empire to keep them safe from attack.

As the Romans left Britain, **Anglo-Saxons** from northern Germany and Denmark started to attack the east coast of England. By 410ᴄᴇ, all of the Roman soldiers had left Britain and the Anglo-Saxons had taken control of the country.

Even though the Romans left Britain over 1,500 years ago, the country's Roman history hasn't been forgotten. In London, a statue of the emperor Trajan has been built in front of the ruins of a Roman wall.

FACT CAT FACT

The Roman Empire ended in 476ᴄᴇ, when the last Roman emperor was replaced by the leader of the Goths, a tribe of people from northern Europe. What was the name of the last Roman emperor?

Try to answer the questions below. Look back through the book to help you. Check your answers on page 24.

1 Which group of people lived in Britain at the time of the Roman invasion?

a) the Vikings
b) the Anglo-Saxons
c) the Celts

2 Where did Roman town meetings take place?

a) the basilica
b) the public baths
c) the temple

3 Poor Romans lived in villas. True or not true?

a) true
b) not true

4 The Romans planted celery and apples in Britain for the first time. True or not true?

a) true
b) not true

5 What did the god Neptune control?

a) the sky
b) marriage
c) the sea

6 All of the Roman soldiers had left Britain by 410CE. True or not true?

a) true
b) not true

GLOSSARY

amphorae long narrow container used for oil or wine

Anglo-Saxons a group of people originally from northern Germany and Denmark, who ruled England after the Romans left in 410CE

basilica a Roman building used for public meetings

BCE (Before the Common Era) before the birth of Christ

CE (Common Era) after the birth of Christ

Celts a group of people who came to Britain in 800BCE and lived there at the same time as the Romans

defeat to win against someone in a fight

emperor the ruler of an empire

empire a group of countries ruled by one leader

expensive describes something that costs a lot of money

forum an outdoor Roman market square

found to plan and begin the building of a town or city

gladiator a Roman man who fought other men or animals for entertainment

import to bring something into a country from another country for people to buy

invade to enter a country and take control of it

invasion when an army enters a country and takes control of it

law a rule followed by everyone living in a country or an area

mosaic a picture or pattern made with small coloured stones or tiles

myth a traditional story, usually about about gods or amazing events

patrol to move around an area keeping watch over it

population the number of people living in an area

public baths a building where Romans went to wash their bodies and see their friends

rebellion when people fight against the ruler of their country

slave someone who is owned by, and works for, another person

temple a religious building

toga a Roman piece of clothing made up of one piece of cloth

tribe a group of people who live together

trident a giant three-pronged fork used as a weapon

villa a large Roman house on a farm

INDEX

ANSWERS

Pages 5–20

page 5: Lusitania

page 7: Boudicca

page 9: 1.5km

page 11: Aquae Sulis

page 13: Some examples include Fishbourne and Bignor.

page 14: Cena

page 16: Wool or linen

page 18: Neptune was Jupiter's brother.

page 21: Romulus Augustus

Quiz answers

1   c) the Celts

2   a) the basilica

3   b) not true. Rich Romans lived in villas.

4   a) true

5   c) the sea

6   a) true